Nia & The Excellence in Reading Award

Author: J. Lavone Roberson, M.Ed., ECEC

Illustrator: Senetha Fuller

Published by: The Now I Am Nia Foundation, Inc.

Dedication

To God. Thank you.

Gompa I miss you every single day. I pray that you still feel my love and adoration for you in everything that I do. Writing about you keeps you alive in my heart, and I will honor you and celebrate you always. I hope I continue to make you happy and proud. -Lavone

To my Mom.

Thank you for buying my my first art book and colored pencils. Art has given me an outlet to give people a tiny bit of happiness in this word. I miss you. -Senetha

- Class Sets and Wholesale Books
- Read Alouds
- Publishing Consulting
- Author Visits
- Gift Sets & Book Boxes
- Send Us Photos of you reading for a chance to win prizes.

Copyright

Copyright © 2022 by Jacquelyn Lavone Roberson
All rights reserved. Published in the United States by
The Now I Am Nia Foundation, Inc., Norwalk, Connecticut.
www.NowIAmNia.org
Proverbs 19:21

No part of this book may be used or reproduced in any manner whatsoever without written permission except in the case of brief quotations in articles and reviews.

Library of Congress Control Number: 2022908929
ISBN: 978-1-7365371-9-0 (Paperback)
Also Available as an E-Book
Printed in USA.
10 9 8 7 6 5 4 3 2
First Edition
June 2022

Contact Us:

@NowIAmNiaBOOKS

Hi.
My name is Nia.
Nia means purpose.

I love spending time with my family and my friends.

I also love school because there is always so much to do. I have fun in art, music, and reading.

My favorite thing to do is play with all of my friends at recess.

It was reading time at school one day. I was a little worried when my teacher Ms. Cobb asked Jah and I to come to the table to read.

"Read this story out loud." Ms. Cobb said.

I felt embarrassed reading out loud. *What if I mess up?* I thought to myself. I didn't want anyone to laugh at me.

I had never seen this book before so I looked at each word carefully and read the story out loud. When I finished I told Ms. Cobb all about the story.

When reading time was done Ms. Cobb handed me the "Excellence in Reading" award. She told me that I would be moving into a new reading group!

I felt so smart. I could not wait to tell my Daddy!

"Daddy, **LOOK!**" I held the award in his face. He was so excited that he picked me up and spun me around.

"We have to go pick out some new books for my smart little reader." Daddy said proudly.

Daddy and I searched through the library and I picked some cool new books.

One book was about a girl who finds treasures in her Grandpa's garden. I couldn't wait to show that book to my grandfather.

Every weekend Daddy and I went to see my Gompa.

On Saturday, I burst in the door with my certificate and my new books.

I was so excited to tell Gompa all about my award.

He was sitting at the table, as usual, with his coffee.

"Gompa, **LOOK**!" I held my award close to his face.

"I am moving to a new reading group **and** I got an 'Excellence in Reading award!" I was talking so loud and fast.

"Wow! That is wonderful! I am so happy and proud." Gompa smiled big and hugged me tight.

"Now, show me this award!" He said in his happy voice.

I showed Gompa the award but I grabbed it out of his hand so I could show him my new book.

"Daddy bought me a new book about a girl and her Grandpa. Can you read it to me? Some of the words are still hard for me."

I was so excited that I did not notice that Gompa's smile was gone, and he was just looking at me.

He cleared his throat.

"Well, back in my time it was hard for black people to go to school." He sighed. "Back then there weren't a lot of schools for black children. Most of us worked on the farms with our families and helped out with the younger children."

"So you had a job as a little kid instead of going to school?" I asked.

"It would only be a job if they paid me." Gompa tried to laugh. I did not laugh back.

That night when I went to bed I could not stop thinking about Gompa. I had so many questions that I did not know how to ask:

Why didn't his parents send him to school? My parents won't even let me miss one day.

How did I not know he couldn't read? I saw him with the bible all the time.

Why was it harder for black kids to go to school than other children?

Gompa is the smartest person I know. **How** did he get a job without knowing how to read? Ms. Cobb always tells us we need to learn to read to do EVERYTHING!

I drifted to sleep feeling helpless and sad for Gompa.

The next day at school I could not even concentrate in my new reading group.

I kept thinking about Gompa and how sad he looked when he told me he could not read.

I can't imagine what it feels like to have never gone to school.

He never got to play tag at recess with his friends or get awards for reading.

He missed all of those fun things.

"I wish I could help him." I cried to myself.

"Good, better, best... NEVER let it rest until your good is better and your better is BEST!"

I have an idea!
I CAN help Gompa! I can help him learn to read!

I could bring him all of the books and flashcards we use in school that helped me. Maybe those things can help him too.

My mom and I pretend to play school all the time. **I know I can help him!**

I asked Ms. Cobb to borrow some books and flashcards.

"Help yourself," she said. "But why do you need this stuff? You already read these books and learned these words."

I didn't know what to say.

I didn't want to tell her that my 90-year-old grandpa did not know how to read.

"I just want to help someone learn." I said as I quickly filled my backpack and my arms.

I rushed out of school when the bell rang.

I had to get to Gompa.

When I got in the car with Mommy I asked her to bring me to Gompa's house right away.

"Today?" she asked. "Usually you go to Gompa's on the weekend? Why today?"

"I have to help him learn to read." I said.

Mommy didn't say anything else.
She drove me to Gompa.

For the next few months I went to Gompa's house every chance I got.

We practiced letters.
We practiced words.

We read the same books over and over.
I tried to do everything my teachers had taught me.

We had so much fun.
Gompa was so smart.
He was a great student.

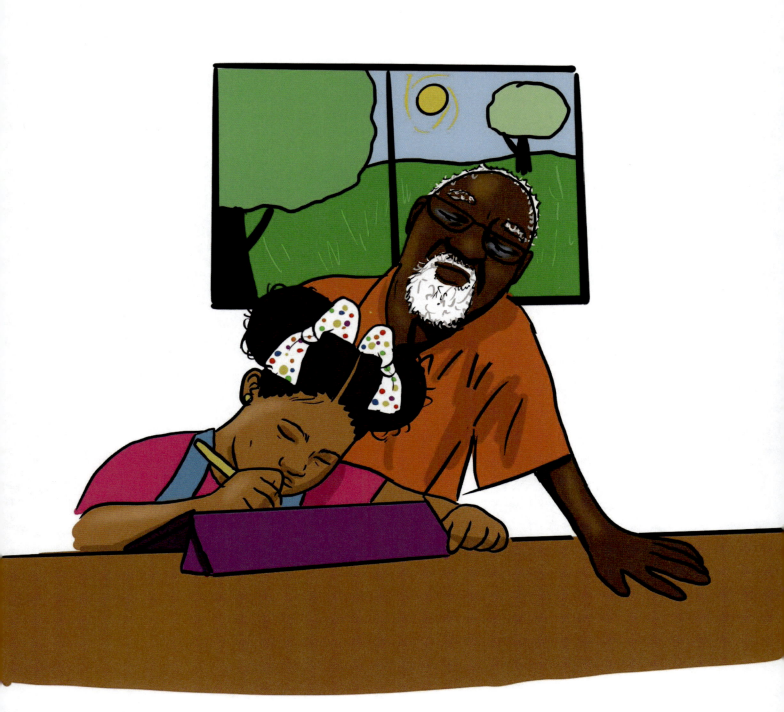

One day in the spring, I walked up to my classroom and saw a sign on the door that we would be having a mystery reader.

"Yay!" I thought to myself. I wonder who it will be.

Last time it was Timmy's dad and he brought us popsicles.

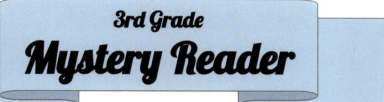

I walked into my classroom and the mystery reader was already there.

"Gompa?"
"Gompa!" I ran over to him and gave him a hug.

My grandpa was our mystery reader and I could not be more excited. He was going to read one of our favorite books that we had practiced. My parents were also there to watch.

I listened nervously as Gompa read the book.

All of my classmates were quiet and listening.

I felt so proud.

I was so happy that this was MY grandpa reading to our class.

I hugged Gompa so tight when he finished the book.

Everyone clapped when Gompa finished reading but the best part was when Ms. Cobb walked over and handed him his own "Excellence in Reading" award.

Gompa smiled bigger than I'd ever seen him smile.

Mommy and I cried happy tears.

We were all so proud of Gompa but I was happy that he was proud of himself.

I could tell he was proud because that weekend when I went to his house his award was hanging on the wall next to the picture we took in my class that day.

"I want to thank you lil' girl." Gompa told me.

"You helped me with something that I used to feel too ashamed to ask for help with. You are the perfect teacher and I will never forget what you've done. I hope you never forget that we always have something we can learn and teach – no matter what age we are."

I was so happy that I had helped Gompa.

Helping him helped me see how lucky I am to go to school. I feel glad that I have friends there to play and learn new things with. I also have an awesome family and teacher.

I could hardly wait to see what we would all learn next.

"Once you learn to READ, you will forever be FREE."
Frederick Douglas

Dear Reader,

I am honored to tell you the true story of **Joseph "Gompa" Roberson.** All of my stories are based on true events. *Nia & The Excellence in Reading Award* is no exception. This story is based on the day I found out that my grandfather struggled with reading because he had not completed school.

My grandpa (Gompa) always read the bible. I would see him with it at home and at church. That said, I assumed he was reading it all of the time.

He was a deacon at his church so when he was asked to read the scripture and a passage one Sunday I did not understand why he was so frantic.

I could see the worry in his eyes.

"Gompa, why are you worried about it, you read the bible all of the time." I said in passing. A few moments later he asked to speak to me privately and he told me "I don't read so good. I don't like when they spring these things on me because I don't get time to prepare."

I was stunned and shattered. I was embarrassed for him which made me sad.

How did I not know that he didn't go to school? He was born in 1929! *How had I not considered what life was like for him growing up in the south in the 1930's?*

The Great Depression started in 1929. Many Americans were struggling financially, especially African-Americans who were already suffering through the trauma of slavery, poverty, and Jim Crow. Most black people were still unable to vote, and many southern black families were still working on the farms that enslaved them. My Gompa was no exception.

Unfortunately, at that time many sharecroppers were forced to choose between education and their basic needs. For many, formal education was not an option. Gompa had worked his entire life. He was skilled in many things and very smart but this day he needed a skill that he had not be taught…. READING.

That day I helped Gompa memorize the scripture and passage but more importantly, I vowed to continue to help him. I made flash cards, bought word books, and my mom bought him an audio bible so he could listen to it. Gompa got better and more confident about reading.

He read EVERYTHING. The newspaper, the news ticker on tv, billboards when he was driving… EVERYTHING.

I was 16 years old when Gompa shared his learning struggles, and I am blessed to share that ten years later he watched me graduate with a Bachelor's in Sociology, Master's in Education, and begin my doctoral residency in Educational Leadership. He was proud that I had become a teacher, and I was proud that he was able to witness it. He loved hearing stories about my students and I loved sharing them with him.

In 2021, at 91 years old, Gompa got sick suddenly. On one of our last days together I was able to share my published books with him and dedicate them to him for all he'd done as my grandfather. I was also able to thank him for supporting my education and for being my muse. He was my first and *favorite* student.

At his funeral the mayor presented him a proclamation for his kindness and positive contributions to the Williamston, NC community. It felt like his graduation for me. It renewed a sense of my own purpose to educate. My hope is that Nia inspires your own pursuit of purpose. I hope this book, Gompa's story, inspires kindness, philanthropy, and a love of learning.

Essential Questions

Use these questions to help readers move to higher levels of thinking by focusing on key details in the text.

- Why was Nia embarrassed when she was asked to read out loud?
- Where did Nia's dad take her when she got out of school? Why did he take her there?
- Why did Gompa's face change when Nia asked him to read the book?
- What did Gompa do instead of going to school when he was a child?
- What was Nia's main problem in the story? How was the problem solved?
- What questions did you have while reading this book?
- Do you have any questions after reading this text?
- What questions would you ask the author about this topic?
- Is there anything you would change about this story? What would it be and why would you change it?
- Is this story believable? Why or why not?
- What does the main character/characters learn in this story?
- If you could have changed the ending, what would you have changed?
- Why did you choose this book? What about it made you want to read it?
- Choose 3 adjectives to describe Nia.

Diversity, Equity, and Inclusion

"Education is the key to unlock the golden door of FREEDOM."
George Washington Carver

Helpful links and resources to discuss the American history of education, race, and racism.

Education

- *The Education of Black Children in the Jim Crow South*
- *Critical Race Theory: The Fight Over What Kids Learn About American History*
- Children's Books about education and desegregation of schools.

Race & Racism

- PBS Kids: 'Talking to Young Kids About Race and Racism"
- Center for Racial Justice Resources
- "What White Children Need to Know About Race"
- 60+ Resources to talk to children about racism.

Social Emotional Learning

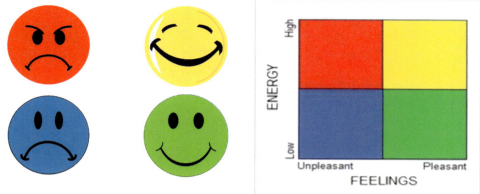

Choose one scene from the book. How was the character feeling in this scene? Use text evidence to explain how you know the character's feelings.

_____
_____
_____
_____
_____

Connection: Share a time when you may have felt like the character in the story.

_____
_____
_____
_____

Mood Meter & Character Attributes

Use words to describe how the characters were feeling in each picture based on what you see in the picture and what you read in the text? Choose a color to describe where they are on the mood meter.

_____

_____

_____

___glum_____

_____

_____

_____

_____

_____

Writing Reading Responses

Use the following to help you write thorough & thoughtful reading responses.

What happened?

- Tell what a character said.
- Tell what a character did.
- Tell what a character thought or felt.
- Describe the setting.
- Describe the important event that occurred.
- Explain a problem.

What did you think?

- This made me think …
- Based on this, I can predict…
- Based on this, I can infer…
- I can relate to this because…
- This reminds me of …
- I now understand…

Author's Purpose

Is the author trying to persuade, inform, or entertain the reader? What message does the author want the reader to know? Why did the author write this book?

_____

_____

_____

_____

_____

_____

_____

_____

Theme

What lesson does Nia learn in this book? Use text evidence to support your answer.

_____
_____
_____
_____
_____
_____
_____
_____
_____
_____
_____
_____

PURPOSE

Each book in the Nia series seems to center around Nia discovering purpose. What does purpose mean and what is Nia learning about purpose?

_____
_____
_____
_____
_____
_____
_____
_____
_____
_____

Pretend you are interviewing the main characters of the book. What questions would you ask them?

1. _____

2. _____

3. _____

4. _____

5. _____

Draw a picture of your favorite part of the story. Explain why this part is your favorite. Label the picture.

Certificate of Completion

This certificate is awarded to

_____

For

EXCELLENCE in READING

This certifies that

You have successfully read "Nia & The Excellence in Reading Award" book and completed the activities.

The Now I Am Nia Foundation, Inc.
Nia means purpose.
www.NowIAmNia.org

_____
Date

Meet The Author & Illustrator

Jacquelyn "Lavone" Roberson is an author, educator, and philanthropist from Connecticut. Lavone is the CEO and Founder of The Now I Am Nia Foundation, Inc., where she leads various projects to support communities in need. Lavone is an alumni of Hampton University and a member of Delta Sigma Theta Sorority, Incorporated. She has a B.S. in Sociology, a Master's in Elementary Education, and an ABD Doctorate in Educational Leadership. As a teacher she was selected to be in the nation's first Quad-D lab classroom cohort. When she is not teaching or working in the community, she enjoys spending time with her family, god children, and MaltiPoo Worthy. To learn more please visit www.NowIAmNia.org and follow us @NowIAmNiaBooks. 1 Corinthians 10:31

Senetha Fuller resides in Philadelphia, PA. She specializes in "urban art" but can create custom art using different mediums. It has always been her passion to inspire through her art. @Red_Panda_Artz

Other books by the Author & Illustrator...

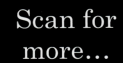

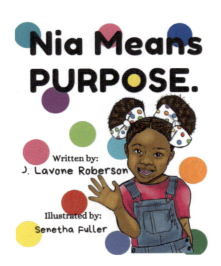
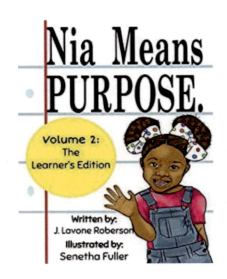

en Español

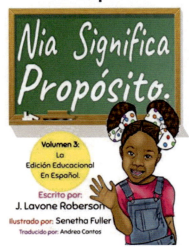
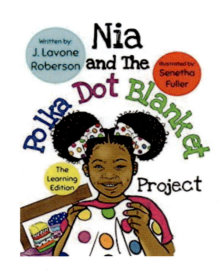
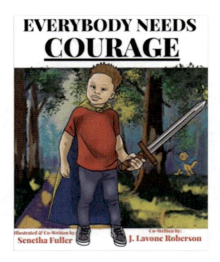
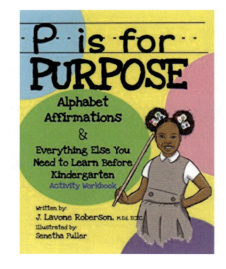
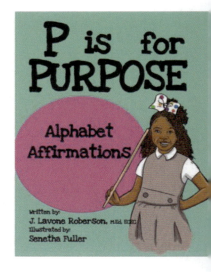

Made in the USA
Middletown, DE
13 August 2023